The Lullaby Book

An easy-to-play collection of lullabies and cradle songs. With words, piano accompaniment and chord symbols.

Music Sales America

DISTRIBUTED BY

HAL•LEONARD®
CORPORATION

7777 W. BLUEMOUND RD. P.O. BOX 13819 MILWAUKEE, WI 53213

Lullabies and rhymes compiled by Richard Carlin
Musicial arrangements by Jonathan Pickow, Pamela Schall,
 and Leo Alfassy
Book design by Nancy Stevenson
Cover design by Graham Percy
Edited by Peter Pickow

Order No. AM 37029
International Standard Book Number: 0.8256.2337.5

Exclusive Distributors:
Music Sales Corporation
257 Park Avenue South, New York, NY 10010, USA
Music Sales Limited
8/9 Frith Street, London W1V 5TZ, England
Music Sales Pty. Limited
120 Rothschild Street, Rosebery, Sydney, NSW 2018, Australia

RHYMES

SONGS

All the Pretty Little Horses

Traditional United States
Collected, adapted, and arranged by John A. Lomax and Alan Lomax

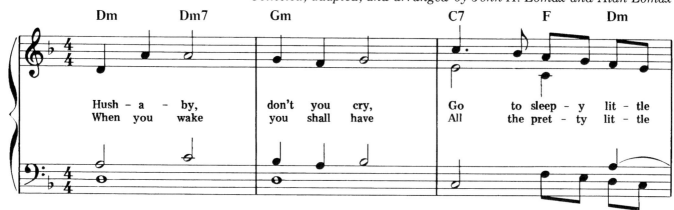

Hush – a – by,
When you wake
don't you cry,
you shall have
Go to sleep – y lit – tle
All the pret – ty lit – tle

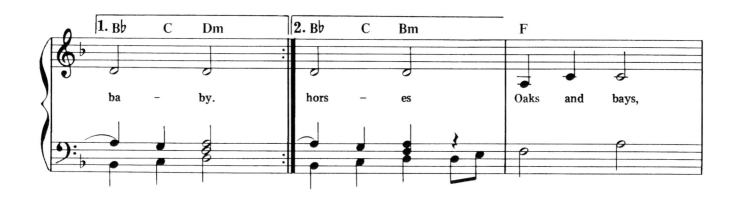

1. ba – by.
2. hors – es
Oaks and bays,

dap-ples and greys,
Coach and six of lit – tle
hors – es

BYE-O

BYE-O! Bye-O!
Baby's in the cradle sleeping.
Tip-toe, tip-toe,
Soft and low, like pussy creeping,
Bye-O, Bye-O!

All the World Is Sleeping

Traditional Welsh

Go to sleep up – on my breast,____ All the world is sleep – ing. Till the morn – ing's light you'll rest,____ Moth – er watch is keep – ing. Birds and beasts have closed their eyes,____ All the world is sleep – ing. ____ In the morn the sun will rise,____ Moth – er watch is keep – ing.

All Through the Night

Traditional Welsh

Extra Verses

Angels watching ever round thee, all through the night;
In thy slumbers close surround thee, all through the night.
They should of all fears disarm thee, no forebodings should alarm thee,
They will let no peril harm thee, all through the night.

While the moon her watch is keeping, all through the night,
While the weary world is sleeping, all through the night,
O'er thy spirit gently stealing, visions of delight revealing,
Breathes a pure and holy feeling, all through the night.

Animal Song

Traditional United States

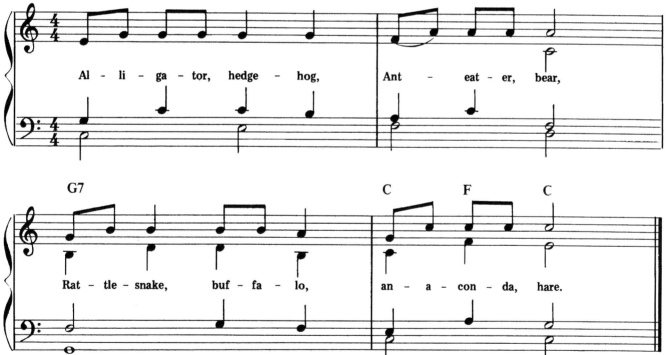

Al - li - ga - tor, hedge - hog, Ant - eat - er, bear,

Rat - tle - snake, buf - fa - lo, an - a - con - da, hare.

Extra Verses

Bullfrog, woodchuck, wolverine, goose,
Whipporwill, chipmunk, jackal, moose.

Mud turtle, whale, glowworm, bat,
Salamander, snail, Maltese cat.

Black squirrel, coon, opossum, wren,
Red squirrel, loon, South Guinea hen.

Reindeer, blacksnake, ibex, nightingale,
Martin, wild drake, crocodile, and quail.

House rat, tosrat, white bear, doe,
Chickadee, peacock, bobolink, and crow.

Eagle, kingeron, sheep, duck, and widgeon,
Conger, armadillo, beaver, seal, pigeon.

Ariana's Lullaby

Traditional Yiddish
adapted by Jason Shulman

Bedtime

Traditional

Extra Verses

The butterfly drowsy has folded its wing,
The bees are returning, no more the birds sing.
Their labor is over, their nestlings are fed,
It's time little people were going to bed.

Goodnight, little people, goodnight and goodnight,
Sweet dreams to your eyelids till dawning of light,
The evening has come, there's no more to be said,
It's time little people were going to bed.

Brahms's Lullaby

Traditional

Johannes Brahms (1833-1897)

NOOTKA LULLABY

IHI! Ihi! Ihi!
Thy father is Eagle-go-high!
Chief of the tribe is he!
Thy mother's Storm-Dancer, Storm-Dancer,
Daughter of the Winds is she!

HOPI LULLABY

PUVA, puva, sleep!
Little beetles in the grass
On their mothers' backs are sleeping;
So on mine, my baby, thou—
Sleep, sleep, sleep!

Bye, Baby Bunting

Traditional English

Bye, ba-by bunt-ing, Dad-dy's gone a-hunt-ing.
Gone to get a rab-bit skin To wrap his ba-by bunt-ing in.

Coventry Carol

Traditional English

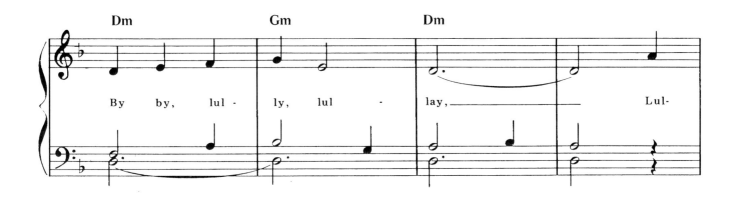

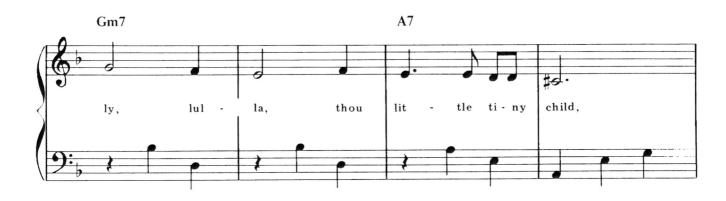

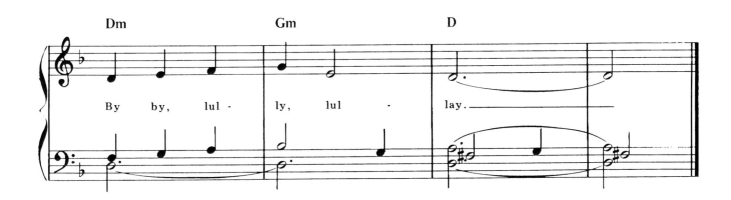

Dance, My Baby Diddy

Traditional

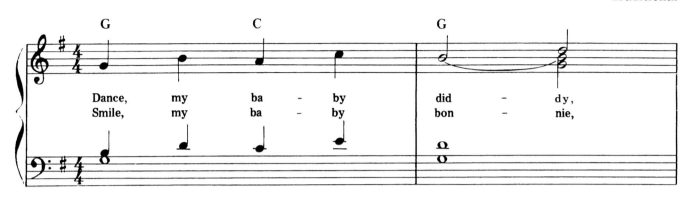

Dance, my ba - by did - dy,
Smile, my ba - by bon - nie,

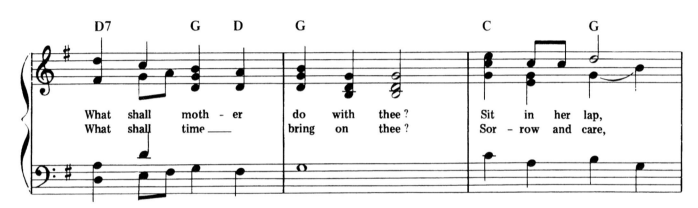

What shall moth - er do with thee?
What shall time ____ bring on thee?

Sit in her lap,
Sor - row and care,

give thee some pap,
frowns and grey hair,

Dance, my ba - by did - dy.
Smile, my ba - by bon - nie.

(R.H.)

Extra Verses

Laugh my baby beauty,
What will time do to thee?
Furrow your cheek, wrinkle your neck,
Laugh my baby beauty.

Dance my baby deary,
Mother will not be weary,
Frolic and play, while you may,
Dance my baby deary.

BABY BYE

BABY BYE, here's a fly,
Let us watch him, you and I.
How he crawls on the walls,
Yet he never falls.
If you and I had six such legs
We could surely walk on eggs
There he goes on his toes,
Tickling baby's nose.

Dance to Your Daddy

Chorus:

Traditional English

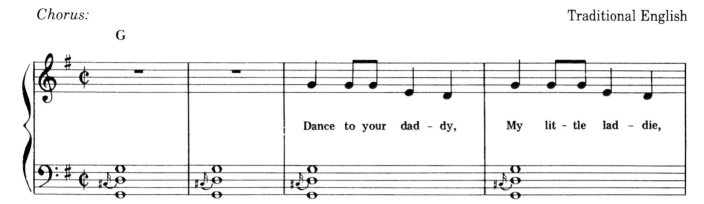

Dance to your dad - dy, My lit - tle lad - die,

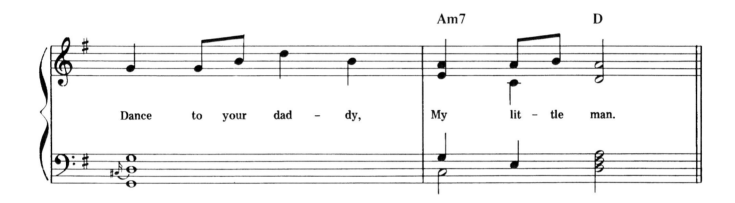

Dance to your dad - dy, My lit - tle man.

Verse:

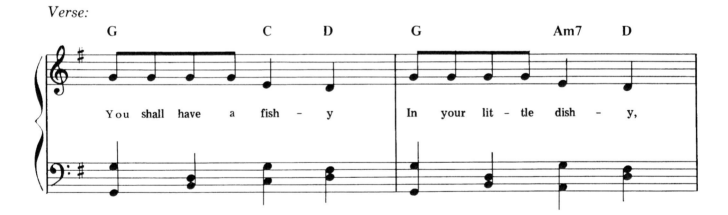

You shall have a fish - y In your lit - tle dish - y,

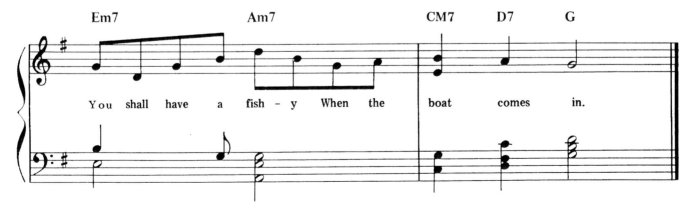

You shall have a fish - y When the boat comes in.

Extra Verses

You shall have a coaty, and a pair of britches,
You shall have a coaty, when the ship comes in.
(Chorus)

When you are a man and come to take a wife,
You shall wed a lass and love her all your life.
(Chorus)

14

Day and Night

Traditional English

By day the shad - ows slip a - way, At even - ing back they creep._____ The sun gives light_____ e - nough for play, The stars_____ e - nough for sleep._____

Dodo, Baby, Do

Traditional French

Do - do, ba - by, do, Now my babe to sleep will go.

Do - do, ba - by, do, Now my babe to sleep will go.

There the old hen doz - es, O - ver 'neath the ros - es,

Ti - ny chicks she'll have for you, If you will sleep as good ba - bies do.

Do - do, chick - ens are a sleep - ing. Do - do, rest, O ba - by mine.

Evening Hymn

Felix Mendelssohn (1809-1847),
from **Elijah**

Hear us, Fa - ther, as we pray,

Thou hast kept us through the ___ day. ___

Fold us ___ now in drow - sy night,

Wake us with ___ Thy ___ morn - ing light.

Far in the Wood

Anonymous

Extra Verses

And all around the little well are seven lovely trees,
They rock and sway and sing a song,
ti-ri, ti-ra, ti-ra-la-la-la,
And whisper in the breeze, and whisper in the breeze.

And through the seven lovely trees the evening wind will blow
And down fall seven little dreams,
ti-ti, ti-ra, ti-ra-la-la-la.
My baby all for you, my baby all for you.

Gaelic Cradle Song

Traditional Irish

Extra Verses

Hush the winds roar hoarse and deep,
On they come, on they come.
Brother seeks the lazy sheep,
But baby sleeps at home, at home.

Hush the rain sweeps o'er the knowes*,
Where they roam, where they roam.
Sister goes to seek the cows,
But baby sleeps at home, at home.

*ewes

The Gartan Mother's Lullaby

Traditional Irish

Sleep, O babe for the red bee hums, the si – lent twi – light fall,
Dusk is drawn and the Green Man's Thorn is wreathed in rings of *(R.H.)*

fall, Shee – vra from___ the grey rock comes to wrap the world___ in
fog. Shee – vra sails___ his boat till dawn a – cross the star – ry

thrall.___ M'le an – abh thu,___ my child, my joy, my
bog.___ M'le an – abh thu,___ the fae – rie moon hath

love and heart's___ de – sire,___ The crick – ets sing___ you
brimmed her course___ with dew___ And weeps to hear___ the

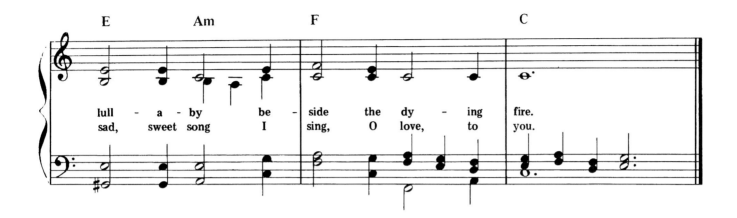

lull - a - by be - side the dy - ing fire.
sad, sweet song I sing, O love, to you.

LULLABY FOR TITANIA

From A Midsummer-Night's Dream
William Shakespeare

YOU spotted snakes with double tongue,
Thorny hedgehogs, be not seen;
Newts and blind-worms, do no wrong;
Come not near our fairy queen.

Philomel, with melody,
Sing in our sweet lullaby;
Lulla, lulla, lullaby; lulla, lulla, lullaby!
Never harm,
Nor spell, nor charm
Come our lovely lady nigh;
So, good-night, with lullaby.

Weaving spiders, come not here;
Hence, you long-legged spinners, hence!
Beetles black, approach not near;
Worm nor snail, do no offence.

Philomel, with melody,
Sing in our sweet lullaby;
Lulla, lulla, lullaby; lulla, lulla, lullaby!
Never harm,
Nor spell, nor charm,
Come our lovely lady nigh;
So, good-night, with lullaby.

IRISH LULLABY

I'LL put you, myself, my baby, to slumber,
Not as 'tis done by the clownish number,—
A yellow blanket and coarse sheet bringing,
But in golden cradle that's softly swinging
    To and fro, lu la lo,
    To and fro, my bonnie baby!
    To and fro, lu la lo,
    To and fro, my own sweet baby!

I'll put you, myself, my baby, to slumber,
On sunniest day of the pleasant summer,
Your golden cradle on smooth lawn laying,
'Neath murmuring boughs that the birds are
swaying
    To and fro, lu la lo,
    To and fro, my bonnie baby!
    To and fro, lu la lo,
    To and fro, my own sweet baby!

Slumber, my babe! may the sweet sleep woo you,
And from your slumbers may health come to you—
May all diseases now flee and fear you,
May sickness and sorrow never come near you!
    To and fro, lu la lo,
    To and fro, my bonnie baby!
    To and fro, lu la lo,
    To and fro, my own sweet baby!

Slumber, my babe! may the sweet sleep woo you,
And from your slumbers may health come to you,
May bright dreams come, and come no other,
And I be never a sonless mother!
    To and fro, lu la lo,
    To and fro, my bonnie baby!
    To and fro, lu la lo,
    To and fro, my own sweet baby!

Go Away, Little Fairies

Traditional Irish

Golden Cradle

Traditional Irish

Sweet babe, a gold — en cra — dle holds thee,
Oh, sleep, my ba — by, free____ from sor — row,

Soft____ snow white fleece____ en-folds thee,
Bright thou'lt ope thine eyes____ to-mor — row.

Fair — est flow'r are
Sleep, while o'er thy

strewn__ be-fore__ thee, Sweet birds war — ble o'er thee.
smil — ing slum — bers An — gels chant____ their num — bers.

Sho — heen__ Sho — lo!_____ Lu, Lu, Lo, Lo!

Golden Slumbers

Traditional English

Gol - den slum - bers kiss your eyes,
Care____ you know not, there - fore sleep,

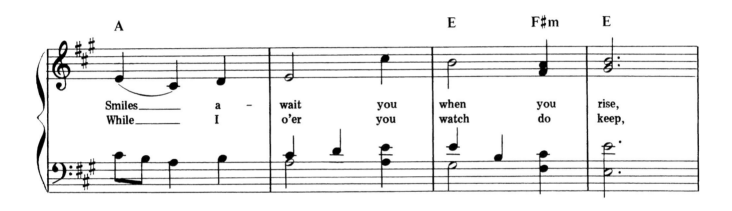

Smiles____ a - wait you when you rise,
While____ I o'er you watch do keep,

Sleep pret - ty ba - by, do____ not cry,____ And

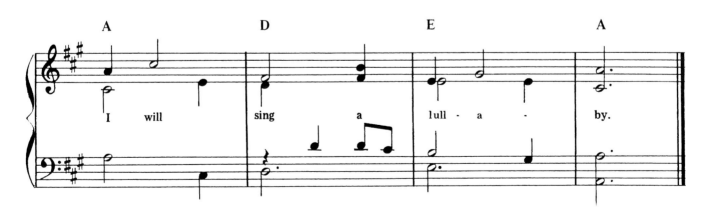

I will sing a lull - a - by.

Kentucky Babe

Richard Henry Buck (1870-1956)

Adam Geibel (1855-1933)

Skeet - ers are a - hum - ming on the hon - ey - suck - le vine,

Sleep, Ken - tuck - y Babe! Sand - man is a - com - ing to this

lit - tle babe of mine, Sleep, Ken - tuck - y Babe!

Sil - v'ry moon is shin - ing in the heav - ens up a - bove,

Bob - o - link is pin - ing for his lit - tle la - dy love.

Kerry Lullaby

Traditional Irish

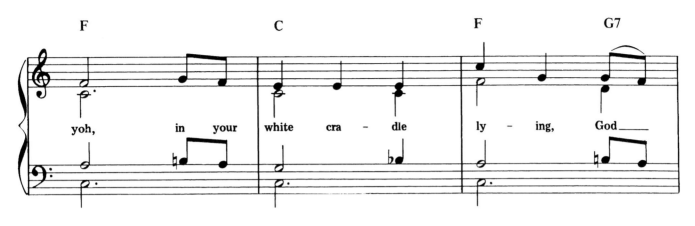

yoh,   in your   white   cra - dle   ly - ing,   God___

give   you   m'lean - abh,   your   night's   sweet   re - pose.

TEDDY BEAR, TEDDY BEAR

TEDDY BEAR, Teddy Bear, turn around,
Teddy Bear, Teddy Bear, touch the ground.
Teddy Bear, Teddy Bear, show your shoe,
Teddy Bear, Teddy Bear, that will do.

Teddy Bear, Teddy Bear, go up stairs,
Teddy Bear, Teddy Bear, say your prayers.
Teddy Bear, Teddy Bear, turn out the light,
Teddy Bear, Teddy Bear, say good night.

Lambs Are Sleeping

Traditional English

*These chords are for guitar with capo on the first fret.

Little Children

Traditional

Wolfgang Amadeus Mozart (1756-1791)

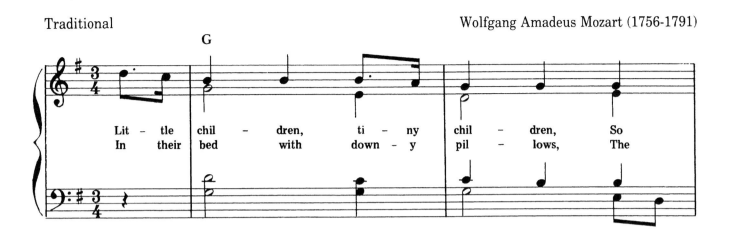

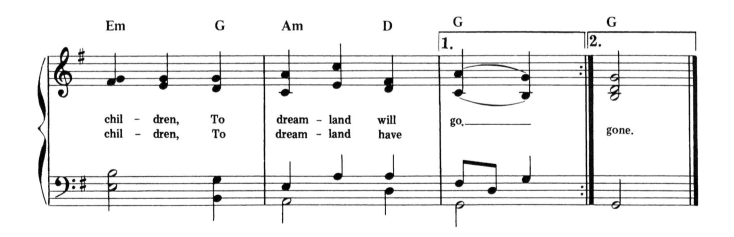

CREOLE LULLABY

DREAMLAND opens here,
Sweep the dream-path clear!
Listen, chile, dear little chile,
To the song of the crocodile.

O SAILOR

O SAILOR, come ashore,
What have you brought for me?
Red coral, white coral,
Coral from the sea.

The Man in the Moon

Traditional English

The man in the moon came down too soon, And asked his way to Nor-wich, He went by the south and burnt his mouth, With eat-ing cold plum por-ridge.

Manx Lullaby

Traditional Manx

O__ hush thee, my dove, O hush thee, my row - an, O__
hush thee, my lap - wing, my lit - tle brown bird.
Fine
O__ fold thy__
wing and__ seek thy__ nest now, O__ shine the__ ber - ry__
on the bright tree, The bird is__ home from the moun - tain and
val - ley, O__ hush thee, my bird - ie, my pret - ty dear - ie.

D.C. al Fine

*These chords are for guitar with capo on the first fret.

Mocking Bird

Traditional United States

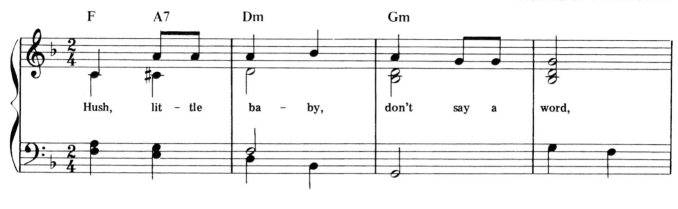

Hush, lit – tle ba – by, don't say a word,

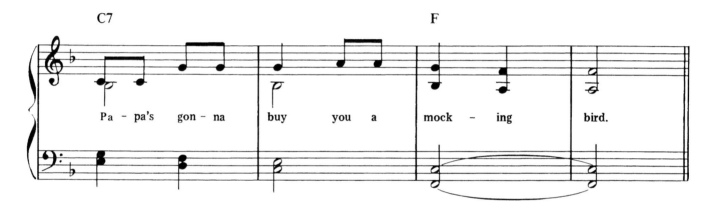

Pa – pa's gon – na buy you a mock – ing bird.

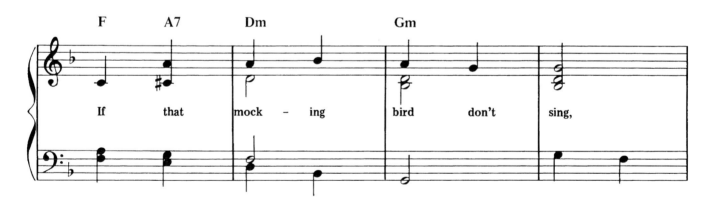

If that mock – ing bird don't sing,

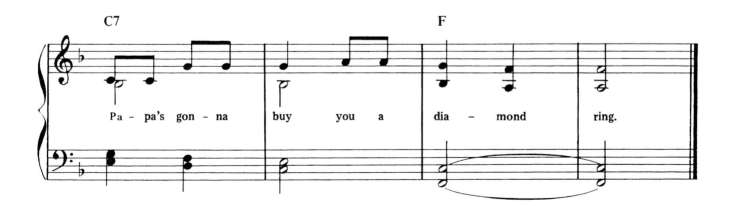

Pa – pa's gon – na buy you a dia – mond ring.

Extra Verses

If that diamond ring turns to brass,
Papa's gonna buy you a looking glass.

If that looking glass gets broke,
Papa's gonna buy you a billy goat.

If that billy goat don't pull,
Papa's gonna buy you a cart and bull.

If that cart and bull turn over,
Papa's gonna buy you a dog named Rover.

If that dog named Rover won't bark,
Papa's gonna buy you a horse and cart.

If that horse and cart fall down,
You'll be the sweetest little one in town.

GEORGIAN LULLABY

GO to sleepy, little baby;
When you awake
I'll give you ginger cake,
And a whole lot of little horses:
One will be red,
One will be blue,
One will be the color of your mammy's shoe!

SICILIAN LULLABY

SON, my comfort, I am not happy.
Other women are gay and can laugh
While I chafe the very life out of me.
Listen to me, child! Beautiful is the lullaby,
And all the folk are asleep—but thou, oh no!
My wise little son, I look around for thy equal,
Nowhere do I find him. Thou art mamma's
consolation.
There, now, do sleep for just a little.

RUMANIAN PRAYER

THOU shalt be a hero as our good Lord,
Great Stephen was; brave in war, and strong
To protect thy fatherland.

SICILIAN LAMENT

MY pretty boy, what can I do?
Will you not give me one hour's relief?

GERMAN LULLABY

SLEEP while I'm brushing the flies from
your brow;
This is the time, love, to sleep and to play.
Later, oh later is not like today;
When care and trouble and sorrow come sore,
You never will sleep, love, as sound as before.

Moon and Sun

Anonymous

Traditional German

Nature's Goodnight

Traditional

*These chords are for guitar with capo on the first fret.

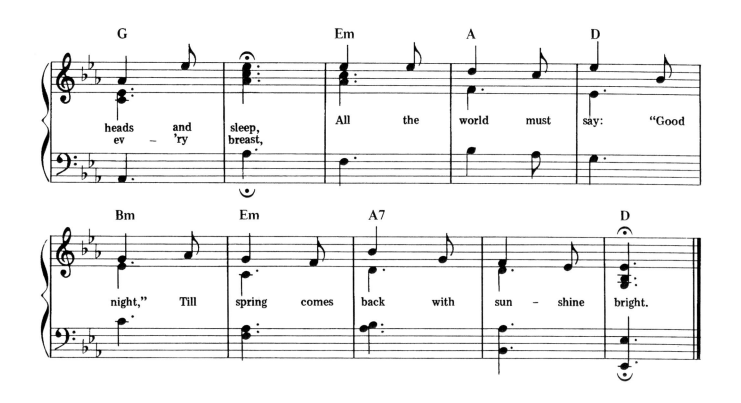

heads and sleep, / ev - 'ry breast, All the world must say: "Good
night," Till spring comes back with sun - shine bright.

Now the Day Is Over

Sabine Baring-Gould (1834-1924)   Joseph Barnby (1838-1896)

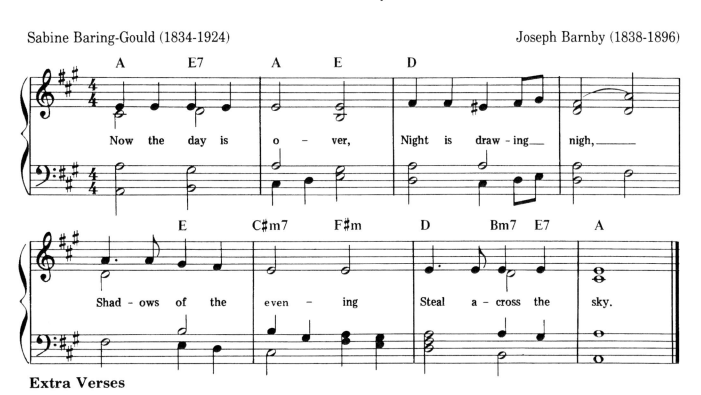

Now the day is o - ver, Night is draw-ing nigh,
Shad - ows of the even - ing Steal a - cross the sky.

Extra Verses

Through the long night watches, may thine angels spread
Their white wings above me, watching round my bed.

When the morning wakens, then may I arise,
Pure and fresh and sinless, in thy holy eyes.

O Hush Thee, My Baby

Traditional

O hush thee, my ba - by, thy sire__ is a knight, Thy moth - er a la - dy, both love - ly and bright. The woods__ and the glens from the tow'r__ which we see; They__ all are be - long - ing, dear__ ba - by to thee.

*These chords are for guitar with capo on the first fret.

Extra Verses

O fear not the bugle, though loudly it blows,
It calls but the wardens that guard thy repose;
Their bows would be bended, their blades would be red,
Ere the step of a foeman draws near they bed.

O hush thee, oh baby, the time soon will come,
When thy sleep be broken by trumpet and drum,
Then hush thee, my darling, take rest while you may,
For strife comes with manhood, and waking with day.

Rock the Cradle

Traditional

Bye low, bye low, Ba - by's in the cra - dle sleep - ing,

Tip toe, tip toe, still as pus - sy sly - ly creep - ing, Bye low, bye low,

Rock the cra - dle, ba - by's wak - ing, Hush, my ba - by, oh!

*These chords are for guitar with capo on the first fret.

Rockabye, Baby

Traditional English

Effie I. Crockett (1857-1940)

Sleep Eye

Words and music
by Woody Guthrie (1912-1967)

Sleep, Little Child

Traditional

Wolfgang Amadeus Mozart (1756-1791)

Sleep, lit – tle child, go to sleep, Moth – er is here by thy bed.

Sleep, lit – tle child, go to sleep, Rest on thy pil – low thy head.

The world is si – lent and still; The moon shines bright on the

hill, And creeps past thy win – dow sill,

Sleep, lit – tle child, go to sleep, Oh, sleep, _____ go to sleep. _____

44

Sleep On, Little One

Traditional

Johannes Brahms (1833-1897)

The flow – 'rets all sleep sound – ly, Be – neath the moon's bright ray, They nod their heads to – geth – er, And dream the night a – way. The bud – ding trees wave to and fro, And mur – mur soft and low. Sleep on! Sleep on, sleep on, my lit – tle one!

Sleep, Sweet Babe

Samuel Taylor Coleridge (1772-1834)

Traditional Chilean

Come, slum-ber balm-i-ly,

Sleep, dar-ling, ten-der-ly!

Come, slum-ber balm-i-ly.

THE MERMAID OF ERRIS

Hal D'Arcy

HUSH, where the bright waves laugh and moan,
The mermaid of Erris is sitting alone;
She is singing a song so wild and loud
To men buried with never a candle or shroud.
Hush, little one, if you hear that sound,
The ocean will be thy burying-ground.

Sleepytime

Traditional

Sleep – y – time has come for my ba – by. Ba – by now is

go – ing to sleep. Kiss ma – ma good night and we'll turn out the light, While

I tuck you in bed, 'neath your cov – ers tight. Sleep – y – time has

come for my ba – by. Ba – by now is go – ing to sleep.

Sun Is Down

Traditional French

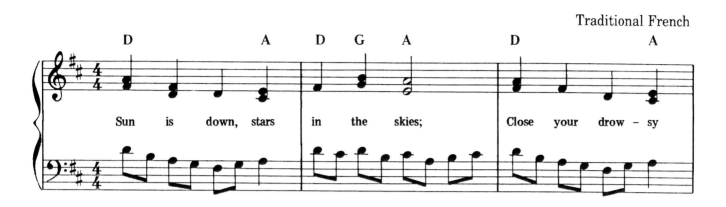

Sun is down, stars in the skies; in the skies; Close your drow – sy

lit – tle eyes. Time for one more song to sing, How

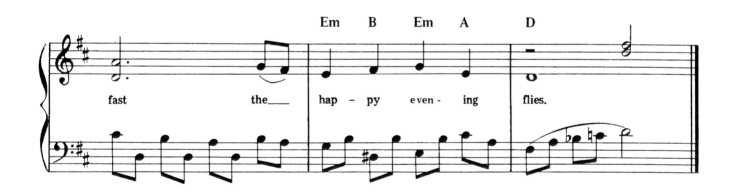

fast the___ hap – py even – ing flies.

RUSSIAN CRADLESONG

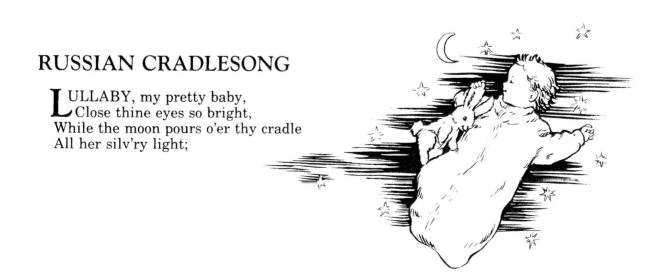

LULLABY, my pretty baby,
Close thine eyes so bright,
While the moon pours o'er thy cradle
All her silv'ry light;

Sweet and Low

Alfred, Lord Tennyson (1809-1892)

Joseph Barnby (1838-1896)

Extra Verse

Sleep and rest, sleep and rest,
Father will come to thee soon,
Rest, rest on mother's breast,
Father will come to thee soon.
Father will come to his babe in the nest,
Silver sails all out of the west,
Under the silver moon,
Sleep, my little one, sleep my pretty one, sleep.

RUMANIAN LULLABY

SLEEP, my baby, sleep an hour,
You're my little gillyflower!
Mother rocks you; mother's near!
She will wash you, baby dear.
Wash you clean in water clear,
Keep the sunshine from you here!
Sleep, my baby, sleep an hour,
Grow up like the gillyflower!

A CRADLE SONG

William Blake

SLEEP! sleep! beauty bright,
Dreaming o'er the joys of night;
Sleep! sleep! in thy sleep
Little sorrows sit and weep.

Sweet babe, in thy face
Soft desires I can trace,
Secret joys and secret smiles,
Little pretty infant wiles.

As thy softest limbs I feel,
Smiles as of the morning steal
O'er thy cheek, and o'er thy breast
Where thy little heart does rest.

O! the cunning wiles that creep
In thy little heart asleep.
When they little heart does wake
Then the dreadful lightnings break,

From thy cheek and from thy eye,
O'er the youthful harvests nigh.
Infant wiles and infant smiles
Heaven and Earth of peace beguiles.

Sweet Be Your Sleep

Traditional English

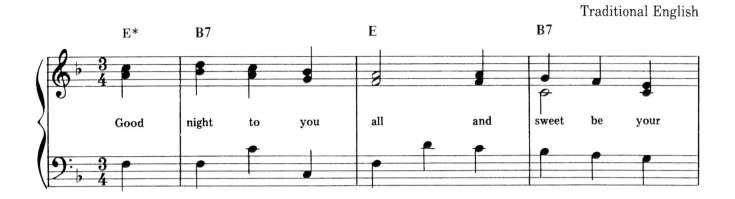

Good night to you all and sweet be your

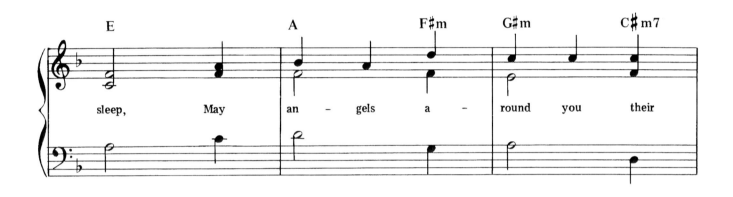

sleep, May an - gels a - round you their

si - lent watch keep. Good night, good

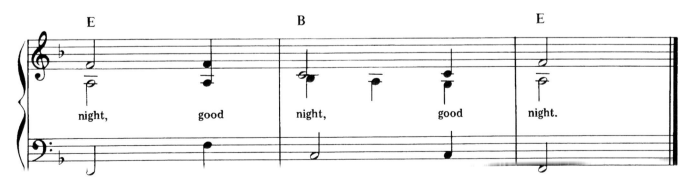

night, good night, good night.

*These chords are for guitar with capo on the first fret.

Time Sends a Warning Call

Traditional English

Tum-Balalayka

Verse:

Traditional Yiddish

*These chords are for guitar with capo on the second fret.

Chorus:

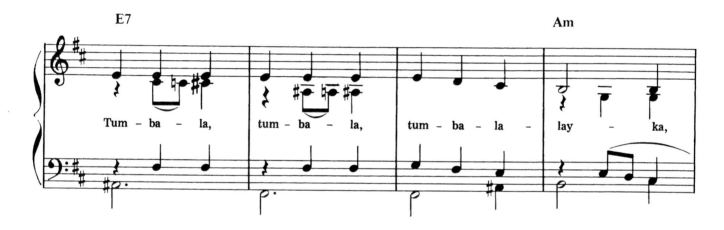

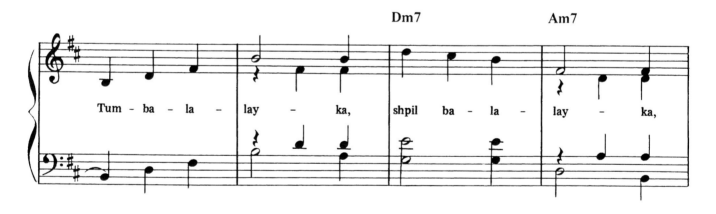

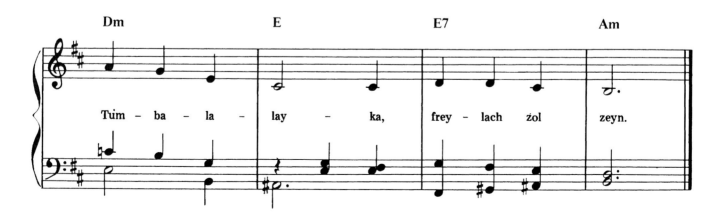

Extra Verses

2 Meydl, meydl, ch'vel bay dir fregn:
Vos kon vaksn on regn?
Vos kon brenen un nit oyfhern?
Vos kon benken, veynen on trern?

3 Narisher bocher, vos darfstu fregn?
A shteyn kon vaksn, vaksn on regn.
Libe kon brenen, un nit oyfhern.
A harts kon benken, veynen on trern?

English Lyrics

1 A lad stood thinking all the night through,
Thinking, thinking, what to do?
Whose heart to take? Whose heart not to break?
Whose heart to take? Whose heart not to break?

Tum-bala, tum-bala, tum-balalayka
Tum-bala, tum-bala, tum-balalayka
Tum-balalayka, strum balalayka.
Tum-balalayka, may we find joy.

2 Maiden, maiden, tell me true,
What can grow, grow without dew?
What can burn for years and years?
What can cry and shed no tears?

3 Silly lad, here's the answer true:
A stone can grow, grow without dew.
Love can burn for years and years.
A heart can cry and shed no tears.

What Will We Do with the Baby-o?

Words and music
by Jean Ritchie (b. 1922)

Tell your daddy when he comes home *(three times)*
And give Old Blue your chicken bone.
(Chorus)

Dance him north, dance him south *(three times)*
Pour a little moonshine in his mouth.
(Chorus)

THE SLEEPY SONG

Josephine Daskam Bacon

AS soon as the fire burns red and low
And the house upstairs is still,
She sings me a queer little sleepy song
Of sheep that go over the hill.

The good little sheep run quick and soft;
Their colors are gray and white;
They follow their leader, nose and tail,
For they must be home by night.

And one slips over, and one comes next,
And one runs after behind;
The gray one's nose at the white one's tail,
The top of the hill they find.

And when they get to the top of the hill,
They quietly slip away;
But one runs over and one comes next—
Their colors are white and gray.

And one slips over and one comes next,
The good little, gray little sheep!
I watch how the fire burns red and low,
And she says that I fall asleep.

Winkum, Winkum

Anonymous

LIE A-BED

LIE a-bed,
  Sleepy head,
Shut up eyes, bo-peep;
Till day-break
Never wake:
Baby, sleep.

PANCAKE RHYME

MIX a pancake,
  Stir a pancake,
Pop it in the pan;
Fry the pancake,
Toss the pancake,
Catch it if you can.

CHEYENNE LULLABY

LITTLE good baby,
  He-ye
Sleepy little baby,
A-ha-hum!

Guitar Chords Used in This Book

 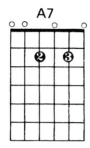 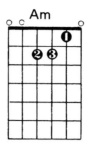 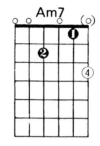 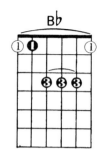

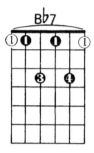 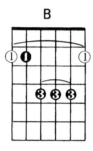 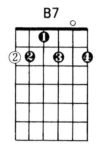 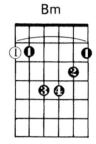 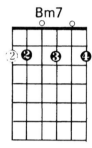

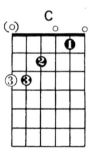  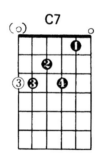 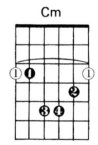 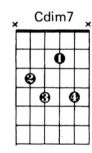

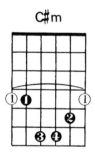 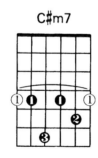 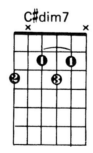 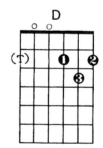 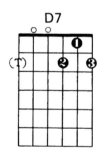

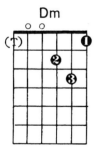 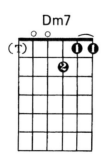 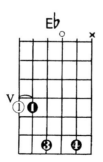 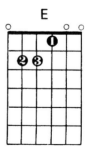 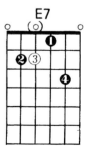

Em
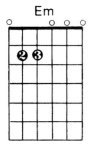

E#dim7
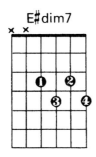

F
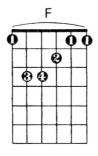

Fm
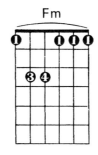

F#m
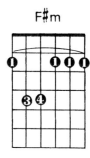

G
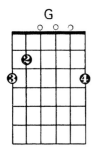

G7
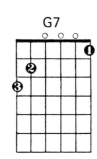

Gaug
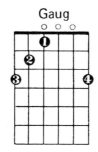

Gm
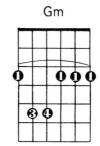

Gm7
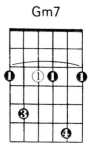

G#m
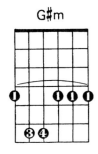

Ab
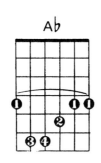

Ab7
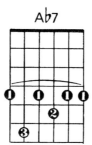